Seeking Divine Guidance

by Abiola Adedipe

DORRANCE
PUBLISHING CO
EST. 1920
PITTSBURGH, PENNSYLVANIA 15238

Dorrance Publishing Co
585 Alpha Drive
Suite 103
Pittsburgh, PA 15238
Visit our website at *www.dorrancebookstore.com*

ISBN: 979-8-89127-746-5
eISBN: 979-8-89127-244-6

Seeking Divine Guidance

Chapter 1

It is so amazing to know that a day will come where we will all wish that something never happened in becoming our true selves. Life is an irony that can bring the best out of us, but not everyone is able to put the puzzle together. We become what we imagine whether we like it or not. It is so funny to know that our aspirations and goals could be a source of happiness to some people out there. Come to think of it, everyone wants the best out of life. If only we could surround ourselves with some good people, we would emerge to the finish line on time.

I smile whenever I think about how far God has brought me with the help of people I least expected. To be successful is good, but at the same time our success is a true picture of who we are now or in the future. We will all be remembered for only the good things that we do to support one another in achieving their goals. Every successful human being on earth always looks for a means to get better at what they do. I would relate this back to the Bible, which says "show me a man that is diligent in his work, he will dine with kings and not mere men" (Proverbs 22:29).

We are all product of our imagination. We cannot alter the past, but we can always look forward to a better tomorrow. If wishes were horses, everyone would be a millionaire by now. The only difference between all of us is our reasoning ability, to make things happen. God has deposited a gift in everyone of us; we only need to look and bring it into existence (Psalm 139:14). I remember what someone said some time ago, that there will be a time when only professionals will be in high demand. However, what qualities do you possess that make you different from others? Uniqueness is one. I kept wondering what would have become of someone like me if God was not on my side. The truth is never farfetched; we only need to be sincere with ourselves in dealing with others.

Hmm, the truth. I remember traveling some time ago and was sitting beside a beautiful young lady, not knowing she was somehow related to me. We kept going on the journey, but the Holy Spirit laid it in my heart to preach to her. I was reluctant initially, but I had to obey. I started by sharing the word of God with her, and she felt blessed with my teaching. Afterwards, we prayed together and I introduced myself as Abiola. However, it was during the introduction that I came to realize that she was my cousin (lol). As God would have it, we talked for a long time and enjoyed the trip together while she paid for my fare.

I would like to share another scenario about another trip, but this time it was a painful experience.

I was supposed to travel immediately after the church service, but I never wanted to go because of personal reasons that were only beneficial to me. I wanted to see my friend and play with her before traveling, which was why I went to her church on that fateful day. My friend is beautiful, intelligent, and dedicated in serving God, while she is also a source of happiness to the people around her. We played together for a few hours and talked about my trip, which I disclosed to her. She told me that she had a sister who stayed around the neighborhood and would come to spend some time with her. I was so happy to hear that, and that made my day after the service. However, I was supposed to take my luggage immediately and embark on my journey knowing fully well that I had never been to the place before.

I procrastinated because I wanted money, but I had some money on me that could have paid for my fare. However, I was told to wait till the next day for me to embark on the trip, but I declined. The money came in as promised but was a bit late. I encouraged myself that I was going to leave because I had an interview the next day. I left the house and boarded a bus that was ready to leave immediately. I was privileged to sit beside a woman who prayed for us while leaving on that fateful day. I noticed that she was the religious type, and I never said anything to her after the prayer. Here came the hour of disobedience, when the Holy Spirit laid it in my heart to pick my Bible and read. I kept questioning him and queried it, saying we just started the trip, that I would read the Bible after some time. Could anyone believe that I never had the time I requested, because we were ambushed by some hoodlums a few minutes after the Holy Spirit was silenced.

I never even knew what was happening while everyone was already jumping out of the bus. The hoodlums were armed and displayed their fireworks in the air, while the woman who sat beside me was just shouting, "Jesus!" We were burgled out of the bus and the hoodlums told every one of us to lie down with our faces on the floor. Items including money and gadgets were forcefully taken from us, but I hid my phone. One thing I noticed was that during the raid, the hoodlums never touched the woman who prayed for us. However, one of them came to me and slapped my buttocks with a cutlass, while he called me a foolish boy. I gave him my money willingly without asking, but does anyone know why he called me a foolish boy? One single act of disobedience.

However, we were rescued by some Good Samaritans who were going for an occasion. Immediately after they left us, my phone rang and I asked myself a question, saying, what if they were still with us? What would have happened to me? God has saved and rescued me in situations when I least expected. But the hoodlums took a lady with them into their ambush while we left the scene immediately. By the grace of God, we were able to arrive at our destination safely. This was how I started my professional career in an unknown location. I got to the office where the interview was supposed to be conducted on Monday, but the interview was postponed. I was told that the managing director (MD) had to visit other locations for inspection.

This made me blame myself for the incident that happened to me while traveling for the interview. I could not go back home because I had no money on me for my transportation. However, I had to stay in the city until the day for my interview. My laptop was gone, and I did not have enough cash on me to sustain myself. It was a boring moment for me, as I had no friends over there. But as God would have it, I went for the interview and I performed excellently well. I was told to resume the following day and start working with my other colleagues. This was how I started my life as an adult, working with people older than me. My supervisor, senior staff, and colleagues were always willing to see me around each day at work. They knew my worth and were not ready to let me leave for another location, even when I had an issue with the operation manager.

This was how I started teaching some kids how to dance in the church I attended back then during my leisure time. The pastor in charge of the branch was so pleased with me because I brought a new aura to the kids' ministry. The kids would minister during special programs and were invited to other local churches for ministrations. This was one of a kind because the kids were given preferential treatment and an honorarium for their participation in any other church programs. So many kids started joining the dance group, and that was how my elevation started. A lot of parents were so happy to see the excitement on the faces of their kids before rehearsals.

It was a wonderful experience to have left home and made a positive impact in an unknown location. After I was done working for the company, all the staff could not believe it when I informed them about it. The staff told me to come back some other time and visit them before leaving the city. I honored their request, and they surprised me with money for a time well spent with them. Afterwards, I started searching for means of working for the Food and Drug Administration (FDA). However, I never knew that God was not involved in my plans to work for FDA. After some time, I stopped searching and started working on other projects that could earn me money then and later in the future. I already had a plan for my life and how I would become one of the richest entrepreneurs in town. But God sees far beyond our understanding and knowledge in all spheres of life.

Chapter 2

I have always wanted to write my own book for a long time but could not get the help I needed from someone close to me. She is good at writing and always helps some of her professors in fulfilling their mission. When I spoke to her about writing my story, she looked at me and smiled. However, I never spoke to her about it again because maybe she doubted me, but I believed in myself. I did not relent in trying to make it come to reality, to the extent that I reached out to Joyce Meyers' ministry for help. I believe that someday I will finally become one of the best authors in the world. I will by no means undermine the value of what grace has bestowed upon me. We can always get better at becoming a blessing to the lives of those who perceive our true worth.

The long-awaited moment is here while the future starts now. People often wonder how I made it through some stages in my life, but all I can say is that God has been faithful. There are different stages and phases in the lives of human beings, which we ourselves might not be able to explain until we overcome them. We do not look like what we have been through in different aspects of our lives because we kept thriving until we are called overcomers (1 Peter 2:9). It is so amazing to know that I have played different roles in some stages of my life while growing up. Recap, bright! How are you? Lol. A lot of people would not be able to relate to that because it was actually a stage play.

What can we say about teamwork? I believe the answer varies depending on different perspectives of the people. However, I have heard people say that love is above the law. Wherever there is love, there is always togetherness and progress. It takes love to build a team and connect with people of different races. It takes grace to stand and win against all odds because God is our shield and buckler (Psalm 91:4). However, we need to build capacity to be able to continue at the same pace and increase it later. We often think about doing things in our own way as planners, but the supreme planner, who is God, overrules all our plans (Proverb 16:1). It might be your turn today but tomorrow for another person. This is why it is always good to do good regardless of your position at any time in life. The travail of our existence is a mystery that cannot be unraveled by human understanding.

Our imminent progression is the totality of our determination to actualize the goals that we have in mind. However, bringing those goals into reality takes commitment and the ability to understand its importance. We live in the moment, but we always look forward to a bright future. Whenever we put grace to work, our life evolves to a whole new level. Our action, passion, and zeal are three fundamental principles that determine the outcome of our services. I remember running away from home to attend dance rehearsals and play basketball with my friends back then in those days. It is so funny to see how time flies and how we have grown to become who we are today.

There are some memories that can never be erased and that often bring us laughter whenever we have a rethink of such events. If you could turn back the hand of time, what would you have done differently? I would say it depends. We keep moving and never stop believing in ourselves till we are able to achieve what seems impossible to others (Matthew 17:20). The grass is green, but is it greener on the other side? Nobody knows. However, whenever desires are granted it makes the heart cheerful. Our gratitude is a result of what God has done in the past, doing at the moment, and looking forward to the blessings to come (1 Corinthians 2:9).

For instance, a young lady prayed to amazing God for a good husband, and it was granted unto her. She went ahead to request wonderful kids, and her wish was granted. The same lady went to God in prayers and said, "Please bless my husband, and I will be forever grateful." The request was granted beyond her expectation, while they lived in luxury. However, here is another scenario where a lady had what it took to be a blessing to others but was more concerned about getting all the money. She hardly had time for herself and kept pushing away suitable suitors who could help her expand her business and commitments. She had forgotten that a day would come when all that mattered to her then would no longer be the order of the day. Come to think of it, have you gotten to a point where the goals seem bigger than you but you refused to seek help? (Genesis 2:18)

A close friend of mine once told me that you cannot keep pouring out of an empty cup. I know that someday when she gets to read my book, she will remember that quote (lol). If I am going to be candid, I miss her because her younger sister wanted to teach me how to play a guitar. If I can remember, the younger sister is also artistic in nature. We were colleagues back then and she was always inspiring me to go beyond my limit. I never knew she saw something different in me and was willing to invest in me for the purpose of achieving my goals. However, she was the jealous type (lol). Never wanted to see me with any lady except herself, but she was fun to be with. Whenever we had a presentation, she was always surprised at the pace at which I spoke and addressed the audience. This was what gave me an edge over others and made people want to listen to my advice and speech.

I believe this is a definition of happiness, understanding, commitment, communication, and love from my own perspective. She knew my value and saw the worth in me beyond the present moment. This was what gave me an idea that love is not something that we can hide no matter how hard we try; it is smoke that would burst open for everyone to see. I kept searching for different words to describe love, but I see it as what individuals possess by themselves. I have heard someone say that love is stronger than hate. To be candid, I believe this is true and it is also a thing of the mind. It takes two to tango.

Chapter 3

Once upon a time, when I was so occupied with a daily ac-
tivity that could at least earn me some money, I met this
stranger in an office waiting to pick up a check, but I never
knew she was married. We exchanged greetings and started
talking about life in general. It was fun initially at the moment
because a lot of laughter was involved. When we were about to
leave the office, she gave me her contact details and checked
how we could be of help to one another. However, I was the
type back then that had no time for ladies. But as God would
have it, we kept bumping into each other at different intervals.
After meeting on different occasions we became friends, and
she confided in me.

I never knew she was going through a lot in her marriage,
not until one fateful day when she decided to open up to me
about it. I would have to say this is a definition of having a good
heart and being in good standing with God. Here comes the

questions that we need to ask ourselves: Can a stranger confide in you? Are you trustworthy? Can you be regarded as a confidant? A friend of mine saw me and thought we had a thing together because he was so happy, while smiling at the same time. However, I had to tell him we were just friends, and what do friends do for each other? With the little knowledge I have about marriage, I spoke to her about ways she could resolve the crisis with her husband. Her dad loved her so much because she was the only daughter and was willing to do anything for her.

If am going to be candid, God is the author of marriage and only he can see far beyond our reasoning. Here was a lady whose father was wealthy, and the husband was a senior staff member working at the bank. But there were things she wanted to do, and her husband was unaware of it because there was no good communication between them. She told me about her ambition and how she was planning to make a name for herself in the health sector. I gave her advice on what she needed to do and how to go about it. She was grateful for my kind gesture because she saw me as a shoulder to lean on for help at that crucial moment. I believe their love life later rekindled and they enjoyed their lives as couples once again. I know that if she ever gets to see me again, 70,000 USD would not be enough to compensate me (lol).

This would lead me to the path where I had to teach some young ladies for free to pass their external examination. How can I describe them? We used to live in the same neighborhood together. Those two ladies are now graduates, and I believed they were married at the moment. What I am trying to say in essence is that we should always endeavor to live a life worthy of emulation. The title, position, societal class, and money are good, but we should be careful how we manage these things. How we treat one another is essential in our daily relationship with others. Whatever you do today is going to be a landmark for what is to come in the future. We can choose to be remembered for either the good or bad things that emanated from us during our days here on earth.

We have seen people do it in the past, and what was their gain? That is the question we all need to ask ourselves over and over again. We need a good heart to be able to accommodate a lot of people. We live in a society where everyone has one aspiration or another, but what can they say about your positive contribution to their lives? Have you been there for people when they needed you the most or turned a deaf ear due to personal sentiments? Nobody knows tomorrow.

Fame is what so many people desire in life but do not know that it has its own flaws. Fame is like a shadow that comes when you least expect it. I would like to refer to a songwriter who wrote a song that says "when he is young, rich, and famous." Everyone would know because he is a superstar, but he did not stop there. He continued by saying, "Momma, when your son gets wealthy, I will buy you a Range Rover." However, can we say that Range Rover is still in *Vogue* now? One of the things that I have learned in life is that no matter what comfort surrounds you, it is an illusion that can be taken away at any time. I will share another song, which talks about all things bright and beautiful, the Lord God made them all. All things bright and wonderful, the same God still made them all. While the song further talks about all creatures, great and small, can we depict the difference between the two songs?

I remember tutoring a young lady for a few days, and she was able to adapt easily to my technique. But to my greatest surprise, she was lost in thought while staring at me and could not concentrate on what I was teaching her. I got to notice that my mind was not with me, and I quickly pointed her attention to it. However, she was not pleased with it because her mind was made up, and we had to stop the teaching for that day. I was not happy with the situation due to the fact that I was already paid for the services.

Few days later, the same lady got to ask me a question: Do I even have time for ladies at all? I was surprised to hear that because I could not fathom why she would have that type of narrative in her. Later on, we parted ways due to some reasons best known to her. What I am trying to say in a brief sentence is that everything still aligned itself back to fame. I think we need to be careful about what we pray for at times, especially if we are not well equipped for the task.

God answers prayers and he is still in the act of granting the heart's desires of his own people. He has never failed before and will never, ever fail. I know this for a fact because my life is a living testimony. There are some testimonies that the mouth can explain, while others are lost in unspoken words. This inspires me to share another story for people to know more about fame. Here comes a gospel minister who started singing for the church, but there was no money or awards involved. He kept on ministering and winning souls for God through his ministerial acts. So many ladies were so engrossed with him, but he was disciplined enough to let God lead him at all times.

However, he was not buoyant enough to meet his needs and wants at that moment. But he never stopped believing in God for his unlimited provisions and blessings.

On one fateful day while going out, he met one of his old friends who was now wealthy and cruising a luxury around the town. The friend was so excited to see him again after a long time, and they exchanged complimentary cards. Unknowingly to him that his friend had become a secular songs promoter, he went to his house for them to talk and see how his friend could be of help to him. They started talking and his friend explained to him how he worked with different producers in the music industry. However, he could not hold back his decision because he immediately developed a cold foot due to the money and awards involved.

After leaving his friend's house, he was so happy that God had finally answered his prayers. He stopped ministering in the church, and his friends became suspicious about what could have happened to him. The two ladies who were always delighted to see him sing questioned his disappearance from the church. But he gave them an explanation, saying he just landed himself a big deal through an old friend. He further explained to them that in limited time, he was going to start earning big money and receiving a lot of awards in the music industry. However, the ladies reminded him of his source of talent, which was God. They asked him if he ever prayed about it before receiving such help from an old friend, but he never listened to them.

He told them to leave him alone and let him make a name for himself in the music industry with other popular artists. But he never knew that fame was only going to lead him astray, even with the money involved. The ladies left after hearing his decision but kept coming back to see if he would change his mind. To their greatest surprise, his friend had already given him a manager and car. The ladies were so stunned with wonder and could not believe it but held on to their faith while they left his house.

Chapter 4

He started performing around the city with so much money involved as an invited guest. His performances earned him awards, signed him new deals with different brands, and he got to enjoy the life that he always wanted. He never stopped thrilling his audience at each show or outing. He displayed the impossible in him to the secular world. However, the two ladies from the church never stopped praying for him because they already knew what was involved. They tried different means to reach him, but he was always going from one show to another. He hardly had time for himself or his wife.

One fateful day, he was ready to attend one of his shows in the city. But something tragic happened, and nobody showed up to wish him well except for the two ladies who never gave up on him. He had no understanding that fame was just for the moment. This was when he started thinking about how he was being led astray by his friend. But can we say it was too late for him? In life, it is very important to surround yourself with people who love you unconditionally. Some people will come into your life for a reason and season, but people who truly love you will never give up on you.

At that moment, those ladies had no choice but to pray and be there for him. This is what we can refer to as "a friend in need is a friend, indeed." They never allowed him to worry about anything but to retrace his steps back to God. He came to realize that regardless of how smart you can be, if God really needs you for his purpose there will always be a way to bring you back to him. He asked God for forgiveness and a second chance to be a faithful vessel in his vineyard once again. Is it not funny to know that we can never understand our God, who is indispensable? God answered his prayers, and this was like a major restoration for him.

There was a time that the pastor was willing to see some people in the church, and he told me to reach out to them. But while carrying out the duty, I went to see a friend of mine who needed my help and promised to pay for the services. Immediately after I got to her house I called this person, whose name was attached to my list. I had never seen him before in the church but reached out to him. I called him and he picked the call by saying, "Good morning, Pastor." I was so surprised and had to inform him that it was the pastor who sent me to him for everyone to meet in the church. He was happy to hear from me and said he would kindly save my number, but we never got in touch again after then. I will say I am not sure if this person still resides in Minnesota. However, I think before then I spoke with my aunt who resides in another part of the state, and she was so happy to hear from me.

She told me something that I could not believe on that day, saying, "I think God has destined you to be the only pastor in the family." I was so surprised but laughed it off. She continued by telling me that she and her husband were also part of the pastoral team in their church. After listening to her for a moment, I was silent and could not argue any further. However, I remember the first touch of God upon my life the first day I stepped on the altar to minister. It was not a funny experience, as I could not stop ministering and ran away from the altar (lol). But after the ministration, I noticed something that I could not explain while I kept it to myself.

Afterwards, I started developing myself gradually to know more about the Bible and God's purpose for my life. But I would say it takes the grace of God to behold and await the days of manifestation. I noticed one thing about myself, that the more I run, the more God draws me closer to himself. I know some of my pastors could attest to it because I was always trying to run away from the altar and do my own thing. But who I am to question God?

A lady who once called me irresponsible had to revoke her words to call me a pastor years later. I know that she had been willing to speak to me for some time now but could not reach me. We used to stay in the same neighborhood together while growing up, and she was willing to do anything for me. But as a man, I was not buoyant enough back then and just started a teaching job. She wanted love, care, and my attention, but I could not give it to her. However, all I cared about was getting money for myself through my services.

I have always envisioned myself to be one of the successful men whom people would like to mention by name. But she made me understand that matters of the heart are quite different from money. She taught me that ladies are able to know what a man is becoming, while they support them with anything to make it come to pass. This made me realize how to love and cherish a woman. However, I have always been a loving, caring, and affectionate person, but my desires wanted to take hold of me. It would be good for people to know that you should not lose yourself while trying to amass wealth.

Is it not funny how God can make something out of nothing? At that moment, everything I prayed about was always coming to pass. I knew it was not by my power nor might, but it was his grace over my life. A lady friend of mine did not like her job and was always complaining about the nature of the job to me. I told her not to worry herself about it, that God would give her a better job with good pay. To the awesomeness of God, she got a new job few weeks after we spoke about it.

Another person was willing to change her job, and she informed me about it. I remember that we were inside her car during the conversation about getting a new job for her. We prayed together about it and other issues that she wanted to resolve. To God be the glory, she got two different offers weeks after the prayer. I know that someday if this person gets to read my book, she will remember that fateful day. This is to show how God works wonders through his vessels unannounced. I understand that some people have thought about it, that is God really answering prayers. He does for sure as long as you are able to connect yourself with him. But these acts do not just happen without a close relationship with God.

I would support this with a song that goes thus: "He never sleeps nor slumbers." He is never tired of hearing our prayers. When we are weak, he becomes stronger, so cast all your cares and burdens on him. Do you think that the Lord has forgotten your needs? Go to him in prayers because he always works in mysterious ways. Our God is able; he is mighty and faithful.

Someone saw one of my ministrations, and when he finally got to meet me he had no choice but to comment. I remember telling him, "The person you saw was not me, but God working through me." I always try everything within me to give God back all the glory that he deserves. Whenever we take God out of the picture, only then can we predict our unseen future. We should always remember that he is a jealous God, Alpha and Omega, beginning and the end. Nothing is too hard for him to do—that is why he is called God.

A lady once asked me why I am so reserved and kind. She told me that she had never come across any man like me before in or out of the city. I was so surprised and could not believe it at the same time. I looked at her with an affirmative answer to inform her that it is my nature. But someone else told me the same thing again, and I could not answer the question at that moment. The ceremony that kept showing up itself was not as beautiful as having a happy moment with one another. Happiness and love are two major factors that will always enable us to thrive beyond our limit. What can we refer to as our limit? When we do not have what it takes to continue the task, we never give up. This has different versions depending on each individual and their foresight.

It could be daring and tasking during the initial process, but the end result is what brings smiles on our faces. Rejoice when you see friends or anyone who is willing to go out of their way to support your mission and goal. These are the people we can associate ourselves with in any situation we might find ourselves. They are called destiny helpers. There is more to life than what the eyes can see. This makes me reference a song that says: "What my eyes can see, I still believe." Everything spoken to me, there is no word that will go back to him null and void. I will trust the report of the Lord; God is not a man that he should lie. Every need, he will supply. I will wait and not be moved. I believe and I will trust in him.

Furthermore, there is a quote that says "Make hast while the sun shines." We will keep trying our best and leaving the rest for God to perfect (Genesis 2:18). Wants and needs are the basic fundamental principles that govern human existence. However, our attitude to the basic needs of life determines the altitude of our destination.